Cambridge Early Years

Let's Explore

Learner's Book 3A

Kathryn Harper & Elly Schottman

Contents

Note to parents and practitioners — 3

Block 1: Places near and far — 4

Block 2: Farms and being outside — 18

Acknowledgements — 32

Note to parents and practitioners

This Learner's Book provides activities to support the first term of Let's Explore for Cambridge Early Years 3.

Activities can be used at school or at home. Children will need support from an adult. Additional guidance about activities can be found in the **For practitioners** boxes.

Some activities use stickers. The stickers can be found in the section in the middle of this book.

Stories are provided for children to enjoy looking at and listening to. Children are not expected to be able to read the stories themselves.

Children will encounter the following characters within this book. You could ask children to point to the characters when they see them on the pages, and say their names.

The Learner's Book activities support the Teaching Resource activities. The Teaching Resource provides step-by-step coverage of the Cambridge Early Years curriculum and guidance on how the Learner's Book activities develop the curriculum learning statements.

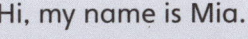

Hi, my name is Mia.

Find us on the front covers doing lots of fun activities.

Hi, my name is Gemi.

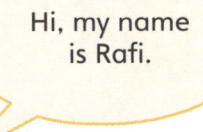

Hi, my name is Rafi.

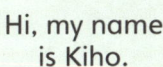

Hi, my name is Kiho.

Block 1 Places near and far

People in the park

Choose stickers and say.

For practitioners
Children explore the picture and discuss what they can see. Children stick the matching pictures in place, e.g., football to team. Talk about what the people are doing in the picture. Ask *What events do you celebrate in your community?* Encourage children to find Kiho in the picture by finishing the rhyme aloud.

My communities
Write and say.

team   town   family
friends   school

For practitioners
Talk about the pictures on the page with the group. Ask *What type of community is in the picture?* Read the words above aloud and discuss their meaning as a group. Children write the community type under the matching picture. Ask *What communities are you a part of?*

Can you see the patterns?

Match and colour.

Find a pattern in your classroom. Draw and talk about it.

For practitioners
Children match the photos to the patterns and colour following the model in the photo. Children then explore the classroom to find a pattern that they can draw into the box. Ask *What kind of pattern is this?*

Design your own T-shirt!
Paste and say.

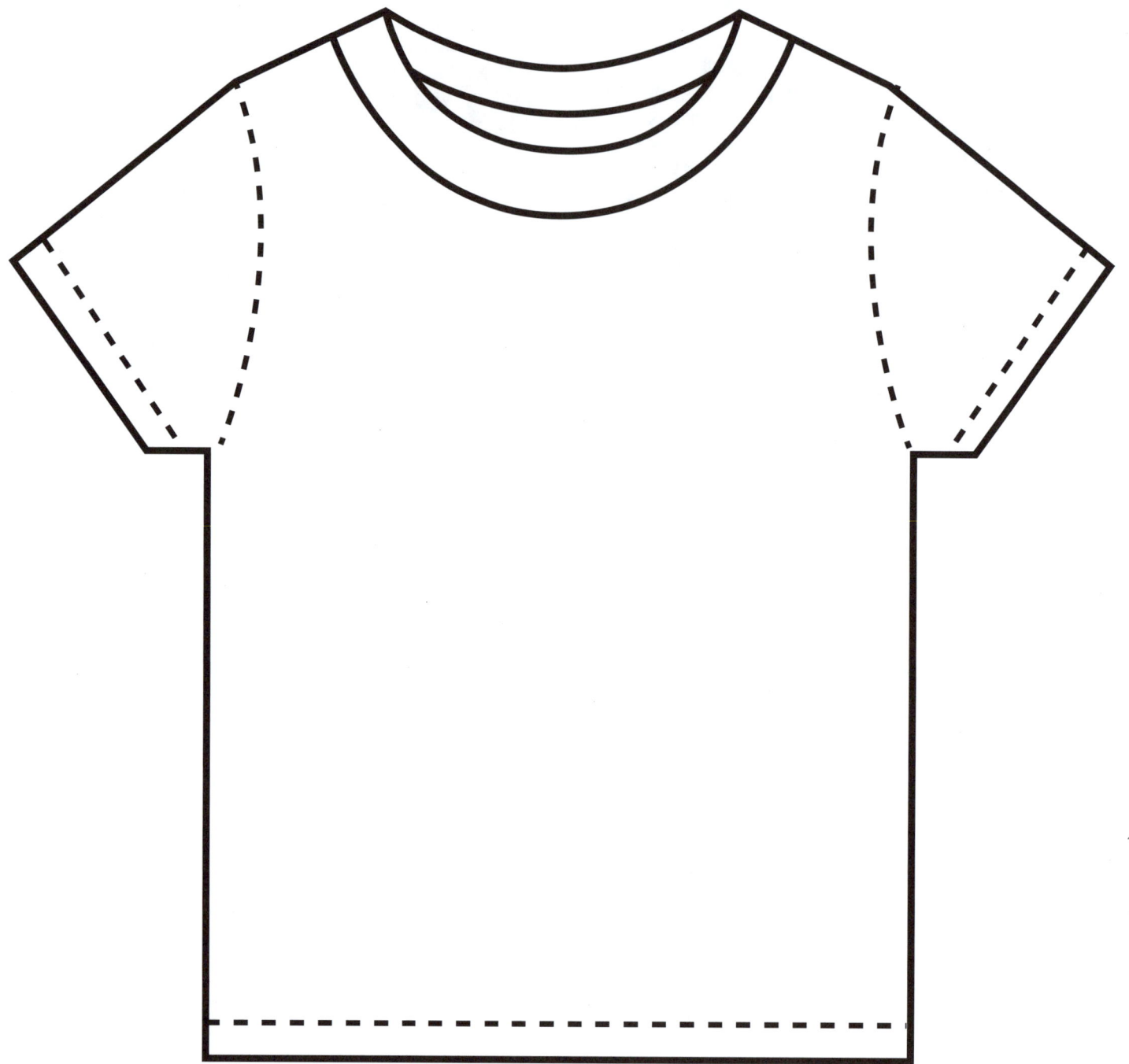

For practitioners
Provide a variety of materials, e.g., felt, fabric, card, bubble wrap, glitter, etc. Children cut out and stick materials to create their own T-shirt, talking about what they use with a partner.

Can you see the instruments?

Join the dots.

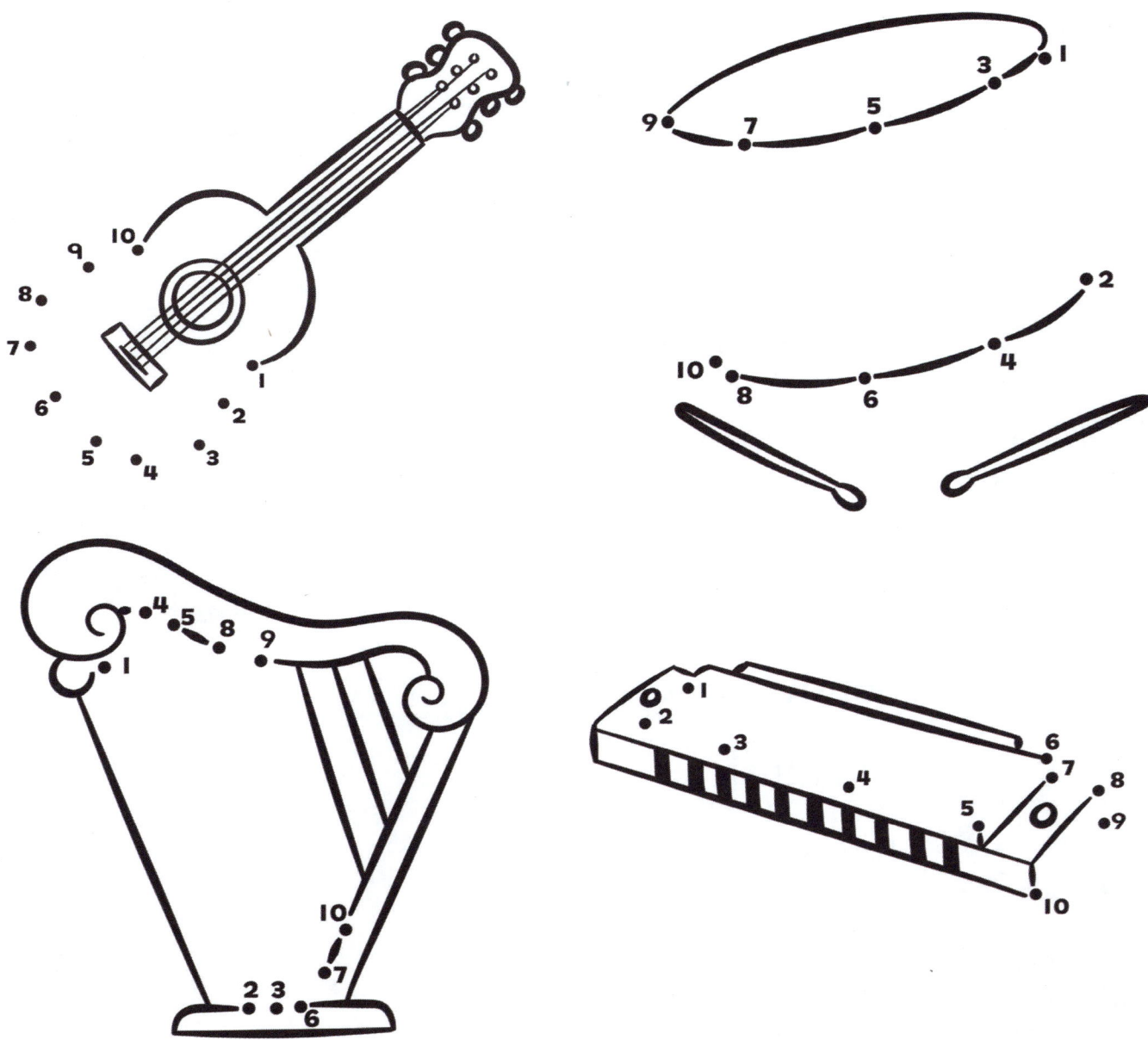

Can you try to make sounds like the instruments?

For practitioners
Ask children to guess what the instruments are. Then draw and discover them. Point and say the names of the instruments. Ask *Can you make sounds like the instruments?* If they need more support, provide recordings of the instruments.

What kinds of music do you like?

Tick.

Make sounds like the instruments.

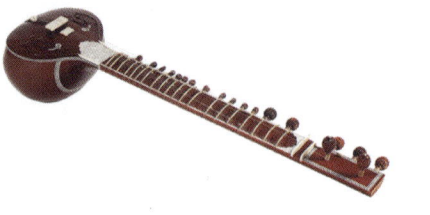

I like …

old music ☐

new music ☐

fast music ☐

slow music ☐

loud music ☐

quiet music ☐

happy music ☐

sad music ☐

fun music ☐

calm music ☐

My favourite song is

_____

For practitioners
Read each sentence aloud and ask children what kinds of music they like. Allow them to choose as many of the options as they want. Compare and discuss their responses. Ask *What music do you listen to at home? Can you show me how you move to music?*

The festival
Write.

1. What is your favourite festival or celebration?
   _____

2. Who is at the celebration? _____
   _____

3. Is there music at the celebration? _____
   _____

4. What do you eat? _____

5. Do you wear special clothes? _____
   _____

For practitioners
Read the questions aloud and give examples to make sure children understand. You may need to offer support by writing the answers for children. In some cases, they might also need support for information, such as dates, spellings of special words, etc. Provide this or help them look this up online.

Making festival food
Match.

Taj and Kai are making food for their festival. How do they need to be careful?

1
I'm preparing fruits.

2
I don't know how to hold this knife.

3
The tomatoes are rolling away!

4
My brother is funny!

 Hold the knife in your writing hand. ☐

 Keep your eyes on the food! ☐

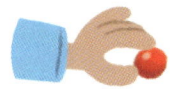 Hold the food in place! ☐

 Use a cutting board. ☐

For practitioners
Children look at the pictures. Read aloud the speech bubbles for them. Discuss what the risk might be in each picture. Children then write in the number of the risk next to how Taj and Kai should be careful. If necessary, talk about the different warnings if they are unfamiliar.

What is important for friends?

Write.

With a friend, work out and write the word.

_ a _ le

_ abb _ t

_ mbr _ lla

_ u _

_ en

For practitioners

Explain how the word puzzle works. With a friend, children solve the puzzle and write the word. They identify the first letter of each word and write it in the box. Help those that need it by talking about the pictures. Talk about why it is important to trust your friends.

The Four Friends
Listen and read.

There is a small fruit tree outside Mouse's house. Every morning Mouse picks a fruit for her breakfast.
"Delicious!" she says.

Over time, the sun shines and the rain pitter patters. The tree grows taller, but Mouse does not.

Then one morning, Mouse cannot reach the fruit.

"But I'm hungry," she cries.

"What's all this?" asks Rabbit.

"I can't reach the fruit," sniffles Mouse.

"Get on my back," says Rabbit.

Mouse picks some fruit. She shares it with Rabbit.

Over time, the sun shines and the rain pitter patters. The tree grows taller, but Mouse and Rabbit do not.

Then one morning, Mouse cannot reach the fruit even when Rabbit jumps as high as he can.

"But we're hungry," they cry.

"What's all this?" asks Monkey.

"We can't reach the fruit," sniffle Mouse and Rabbit.

"I can climb up the tree," says Monkey. He climbs up the tree and drops some fruit to Rabbit and Mouse.

Over time, the sun shines and the rain pitter patters. The tree grows even taller. The storms come and the winds blow. Monkey falls out of the tree and hurts his arm.

"Ouch! I can't climb," he says. They all start to cry.

"What's all this?" asks Elephant.

"We can't reach the fruit and we're hungry," says Mouse, Rabbit and Monkey.

"It's very high up," says Elephant. "I can't reach it … hmmmm … I know! Monkey can climb on my back. Rabbit can climb on Monkey's back. Mouse can climb on Rabbit's back."

"And I can pick the fruit!" squeaks Mouse.

That is what they do. Then they share all the fruit and have a lovely breakfast.

For practitioners

Ask children to find the words for the four friends and say them. Read the story aloud. Children think about the characters in the story. Ask *What does monkey say to his friends? What kind of voice does he have? How does he feel in the story?*

Who's your favourite character?

Draw.

Draw your favourite character.
How would they answer the questions?

What's your name? _____

Are you big or small? _____

Do you move slow or fast? _____

For practitioners
Children choose a character to draw. They complete and act out an interview with their character. They think about how it talks and moves.

Stickers for pages 4–5

Stickers for pages 18-19

Stickers for page 23

Who does these things?
Circle.

Celebrate a wedding together.  teams    families

Celebrate a festival together.  families    country

Celebrate scoring a goal.  teams    country

Eat special foods together.  teams   families

Make bracelets for each other.  friends    teams

Help each other.   friends   families

For practitioners
Read the sentences together to ensure children understand them. Children circle the picture they feel is most appropriate to the sentence. Tell them the answers can vary and they can circle more than one picture. Children can discuss other possible answers for each sentence. This activity is a summary and reflection of the topic and can act as the start of a discussion and the sharing of experiences.

Block 2 — Farms and being outside

On the farm
Choose stickers and say.

18

From seed to plant

Draw and write.

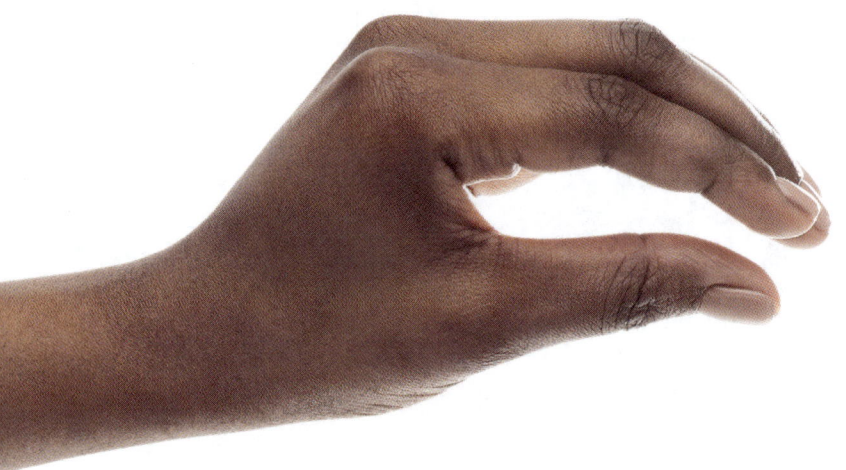

Name of my plant _____

> **For practitioners**
> Children draw a seed held in the child's fingers. They draw a plant that will grow from that seed. Brainstorm ideas together to spark imaginations, or suggest children using books to draw inspiration from. It can be a real or fantasy plant. Children write the name of their plant. Ask *How will you help your plant grow big and strong?*

Parts of a plant
Look and colour.

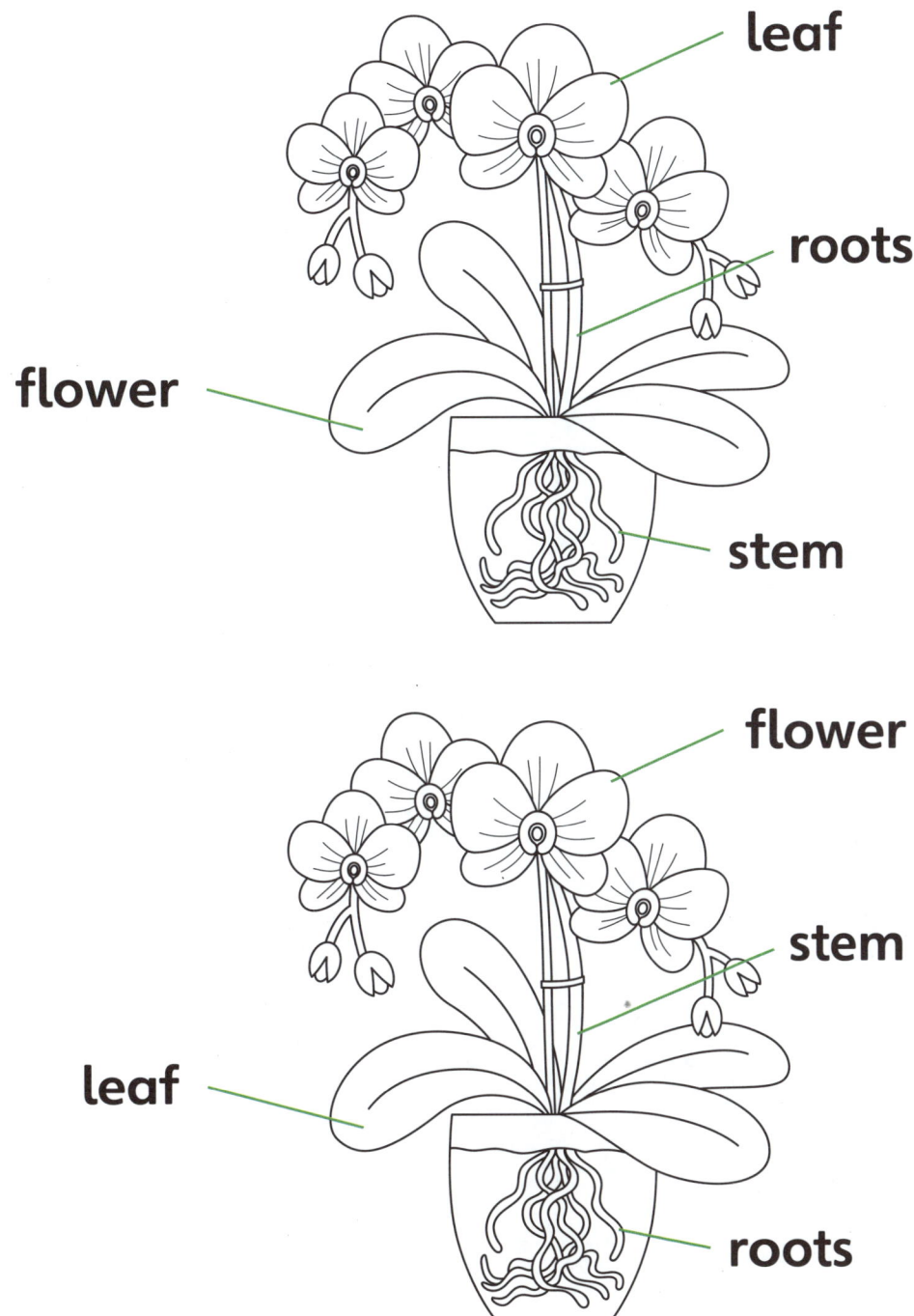

For practitioners

Explain that one of the orchids has been labelled incorrectly. Children identify the orchid with the correct labelling and they colour it in. You will need to offer support with reading each word for this activity. They can colour the incorrect one in any colours they wish. Show some real plants to children and ask them to name their parts.

Watch the pea plant grow!

Draw.

Draw a path through the maze.
Hint: Look for the pictures that show how the plant grows.

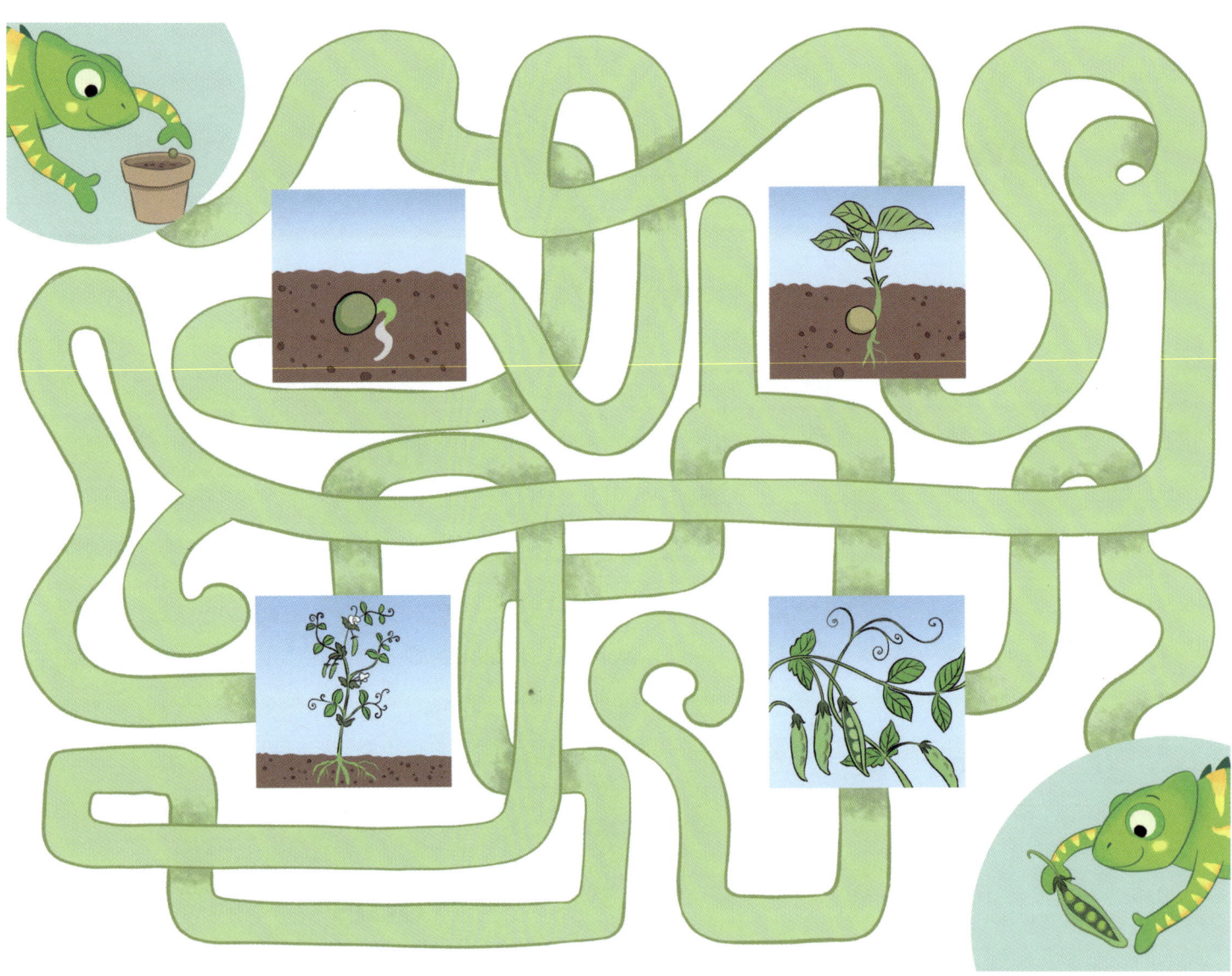

For practitioners

Discuss the pictures of Kiho the chameleon at the start and end of the maze, and the sequence pictures of the growing pea plant inside the maze. Children can use their finger first to find the path through the maze before using a pencil to trace the route.

Living or not living?

Choose stickers and say.

Sort and draw.

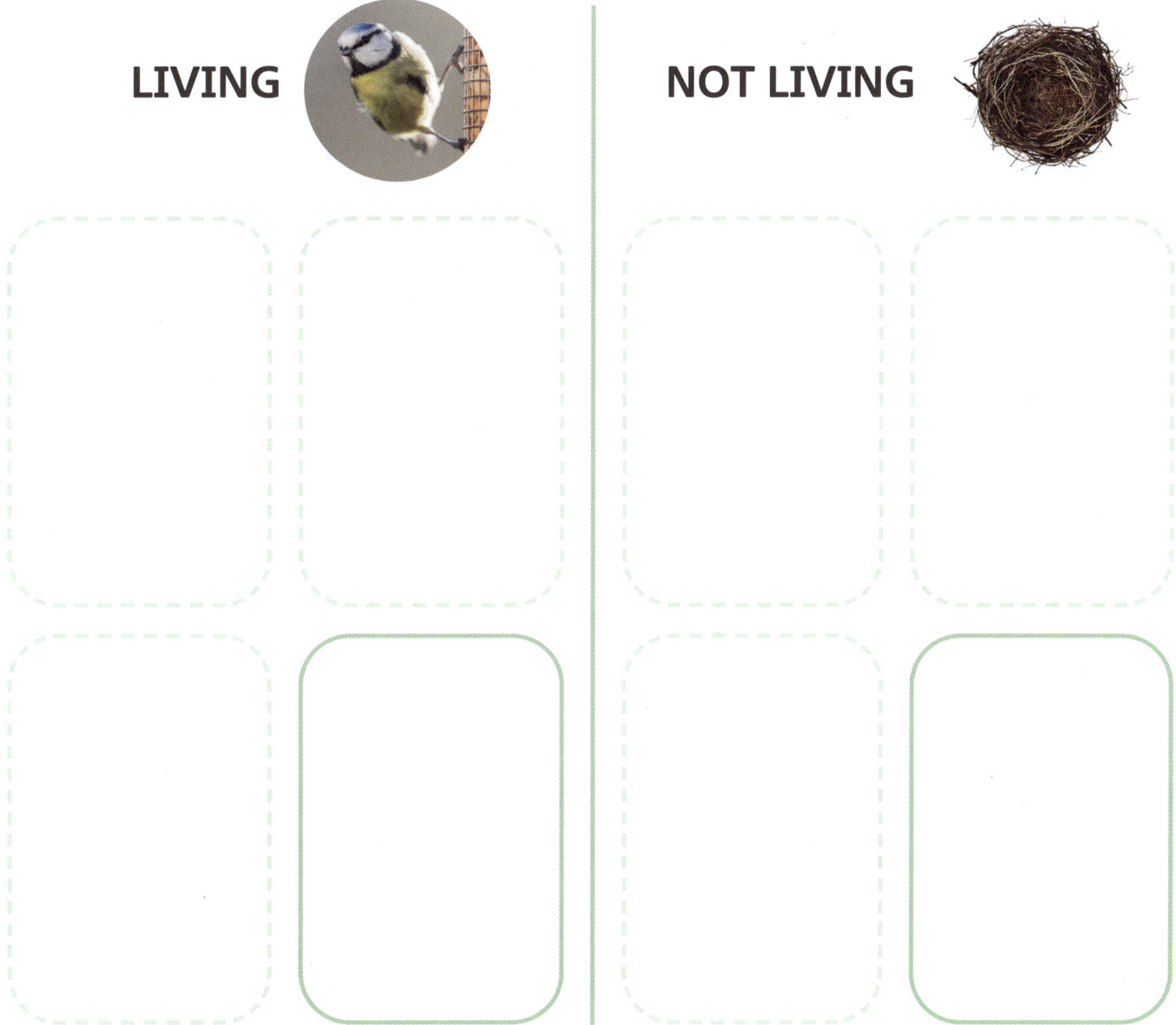

LIVING | NOT LIVING

For practitioners

Children preview the stickers and the chart and talk about what living things have in common. They work in small groups to place the stickers in the correct column then draw a living thing and a non-living thing of their choice at the bottom of the columns.

23

What living things need

Draw.

Listen, read and draw.

All living things need water.
Plants need water.

Animals need water.
People need water too.

All living things need air.
Take a deep breath.

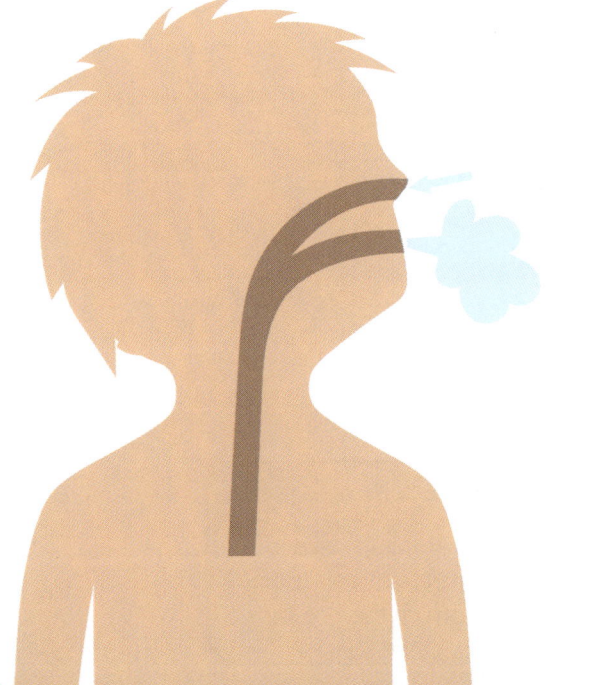

All living things need food.
Different animals eat different food.

What do you like to eat?

For practitioners

Read the text aloud and children read along. Ask questions to prompt children to gather information and think more deeply about the topic, e.g., *What happens to plants when they do not get water? How can plants get water when it does not rain?* Share their responses.

Busy ants

Sing.

Sing and write.

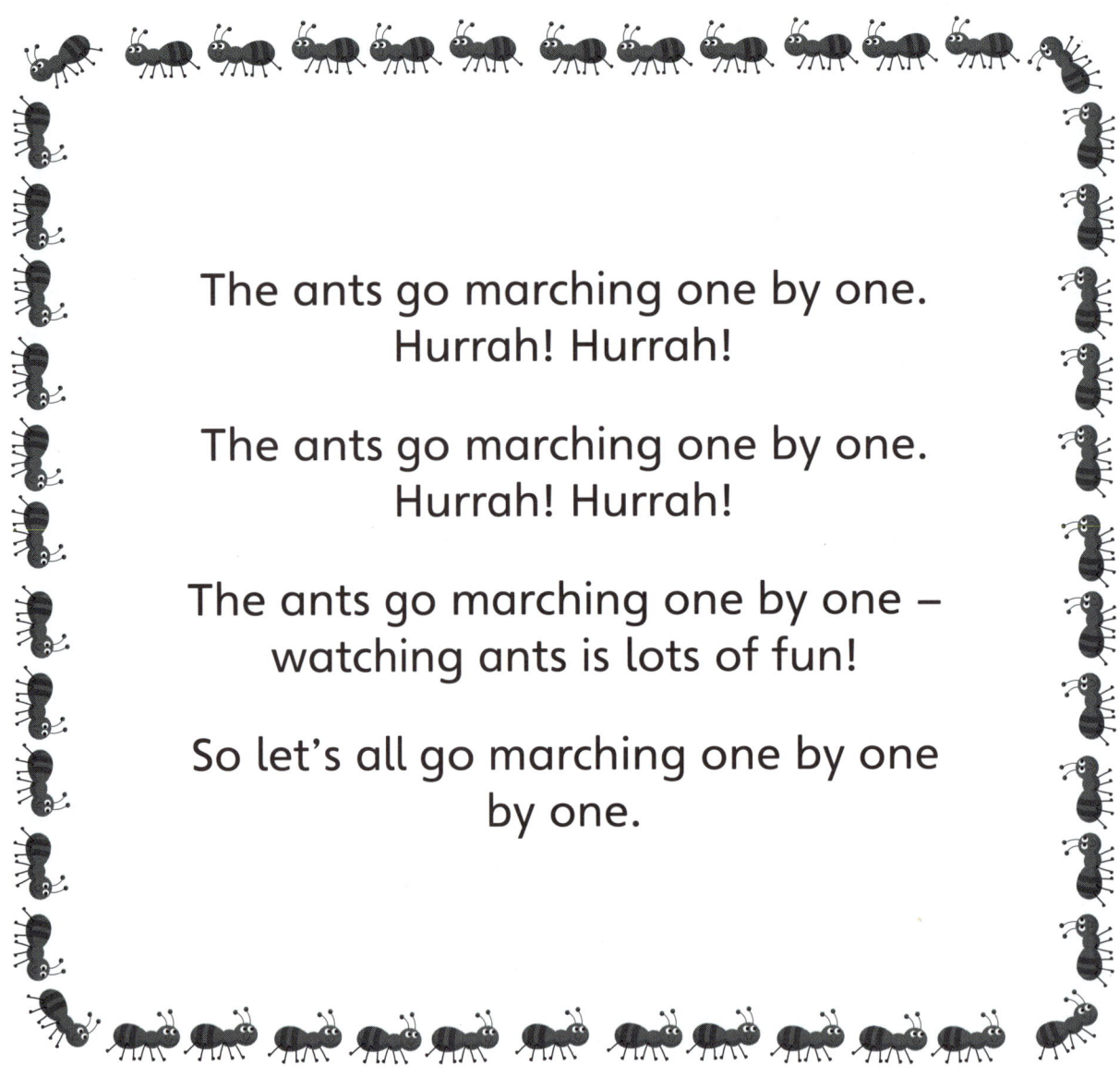

The ants go marching one by one.
Hurrah! Hurrah!

The ants go marching one by one.
Hurrah! Hurrah!

The ants go marching one by one –
watching ants is lots of fun!

So let's all go marching one by one
by one.

Ants can _____.

For practitioners
Sing the song then have children recall things they have seen ants do, either first-hand or in books or videos. Children then write a fact about what ants can do and share this with a classmate.

Thank you, animals!
Match.

Some farms raise special caterpillars called silkworms. Silkworms make silk!

For practitioners
Help children make connections, e.g., *Has anyone eaten honey? What other farm animals lay eggs? Is anyone wearing something made of wool?* Children work in small groups/pairs. They identify the animals and draw a line to the product that comes from that animal. Ask *Can you move and make sounds like each animal?*

2 legs, 4 legs, 6 legs
Match.

For practitioners
Children draw lines to classify animals by the number of legs each animal has.

Colourful fruits and vegetables

Draw.

Draw pictures in the stripes.

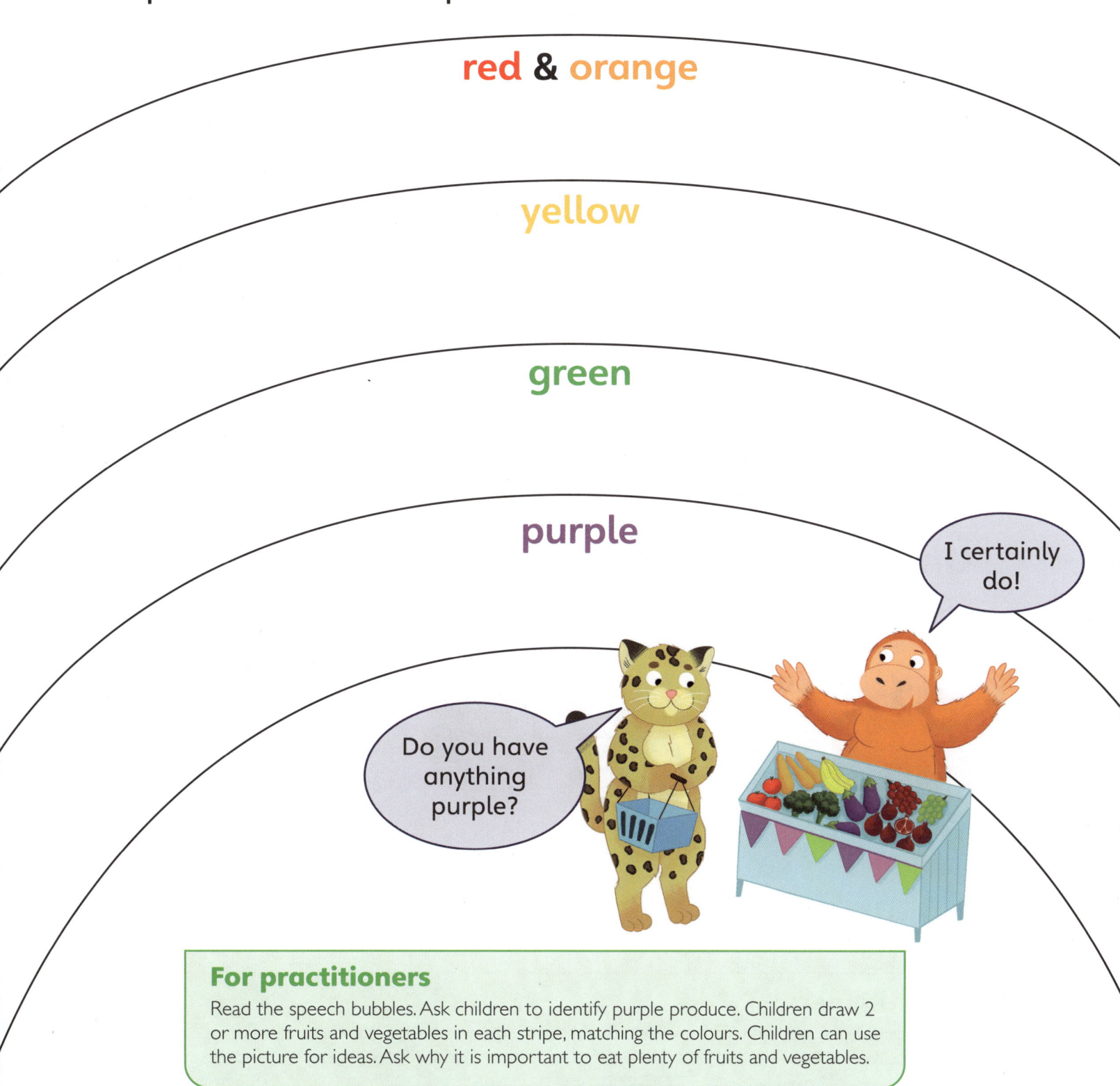

For practitioners

Read the speech bubbles. Ask children to identify purple produce. Children draw 2 or more fruits and vegetables in each stripe, matching the colours. Children can use the picture for ideas. Ask why it is important to eat plenty of fruits and vegetables.

Where do they grow?

Match.

Above the ground

Under the ground

Onion

Mangoes

Peas

Tomato

Potato

Cherries

For practitioners
Read the coloured labels with children and help them identify the photos. Explain the task. Encourage children to work together to decide where each food item grows and draw a line between the picture and the correct label.

What do you like to do?

Think and colour.

 Yes! I like it.

 It's OK.

 I don't like it.

Learning about animals

Growing plants

Singing songs and dancing

Drawing and painting

Working with a group of friends

Working alone

For practitioners
Read the statements aloud and pause for children to colour the face of their choice. This is an opportunity for children to think about their experiences from this topic and share their preferences with you and their classmates.

Acknowledgements

The authors and publishers acknowledge the following sources of copyright material and are grateful for the permissions granted.
While every effort has been made, it has not always been possible to identify the sources of all the material used, or to trace all copyright holders.
If any omissions are brought to our notice, we will be happy to include the appropriate acknowledgements on reprinting.

Thanks to the following for permission to reproduce images:

p6 Userba011d64_201/GI; FatCamera/GI; Image Source/GI; JohnnyGreig/GI; Buena Vista Images/GI; FatCamera/GI; p7 Ihor Reshetniak/GI; D things/GI; Adrienne Bresnahan/GI; Chuchart duangdaw/GI; RobinOlimb/GI; p10 YinYang/GI; IndiaPix/IndiaPicture/GI; Artpartner-images/GI; Phant/GI; Bob Jacobson/GI; Fuse/GI; Mokuden-photos/GI; Tuul & Bruno Morandi/GI; p11 Faidzzainal/GI; mattabbe/GI; Nikola Stojadinovic/GI; Buena Vista Images/GI; p13 Nednapa Chumjumpa/GI; Kaphoto/GI; Howard Kingsnorth/GI; JuliarStudio/GI; Flowgraph/GI; p20 Prostock-Studio/GI; Rocter/GI; p23 James Warwick/GI; Sean Gladwell/GI; (stickers: Stockphotosart/GI; Lezh/GI; Alasdairjames/GI; Luc TEBOUL/GI; vusta/GI; Antpkr/GI); p27 Darios44/GI; Jimmylung/GI; Patricia Hamilton/GI; R-J-Seymour/GI; Santje09/GI; Ljupco/GI; Richard Villalonundefined undefined/GI; Pepifoto/GI; p30 Mariusfm77/GI; Photomaru/GI; Chengyuzheng/GI; Taras Dovhych/GI; Michael Reinhard/GI; Alinamd/GI

Key: GI = Getty Images

Thanks to the following artists at Beehive Illustration:

Laura Arias, Lays Bittencourt, Helen Graper, Tamara Joubert, John Lund, Nathalie Ortega, Sarah Pitt, Jan Smith.

Cover characters by Becky Davies (The Bright Agency)